A Hat for Pat

by Dianne Irving
illustrated by Simon Scales

Harcourt
SCHOOL PUBLISHERS

Printed in China

ISBN 10: 0-15-351217-2
ISBN 13: 978-0-15-351217-9

Ordering Options
ISBN 10: 0-15-351211-3 (Grade 1 Advanced Collection)
ISBN 13: 978-0-15-351211-7 (Grade 1 Advanced Collection)
ISBN 10: 0-15-358014-3 (package of 5)
ISBN 13: 978-0-15-358014-7 (package of 5)

4 5 6 7 8 9 10   0940   15 14 13 12 11 10 09

Pat can make a hat.

We can all help him.

Here is a bag.

Here is a rag.

Here is a fan.

Now let's make it.

Look at the hat for Pat!